A Bare Bones
Review
in US History
and Government.

Daniel E. Meier

ISBN 978-1-4116-8093-7

Published 2006 at LULU.com
No reproduction without author's permission.

Cover Photo by Mike Weber

A Bare Bones
A Review in
US History and Government.
by Daniel E. Meier

Table of Contents

Themes in US History and Government.

Equality

Territorial Expansion

Constitutional Principles

Social Change

Foreign Policy

Constitutional Change/Amendments

Geography and US Government Actions

Reform Movements

Cold War

Presidential Actions

Science and Technology

Controversies

Diversity

Environment and Society

Unit
Highlights

<u>Highlights</u>
<u>Unit I: Discovery to Revolution.</u>

<u>Important People:</u>

Christopher Columbus

John Winthrop: What document did he help to create?

John Smith

Thomas Jefferson

John Adams

Thomas Paine: Identify two key publications he authored?

George Washington: What are the three reasons he is known as "The Father of our Country?"

Concepts:

Salutary Neglect

Interdependence

Triangular Trade

Mercantilism

Imperialism

Documents:

Mayflower Compact

Declaratory Act

Common Sense

Declaration of Independence

Treaty of Paris 1783

Connections:

Describe two examples of how geography impacted the ...

    Development of Native Cultures

    Development of American Colonies

Define Mercantilism and show how it applies to triangular trade.

Much of the "Declaration of Independence" is based on British Philosopher John Locke and his concept of Natural Rights. What are they and how where they used?

In what ways did the events of the Revolutionary Era greatly impact the writing of the US Constitution?

Highlights
Unit II: Government.

Important People:

Alexander Hamilton: What key set of documents did he publish? What was the key theme of those documents?

John Locke: How did his work influence the US Constitution?

Rousseau: How did his work influence the US Constitution?

Montesquieu: How did his work influence the US Constitution?

Voltaire: How did his work influence the US Constitution?

Concepts:

Federalism:

Separation of Powers: Identify *three* ways the US Constitution separates power.

Checks and Balances:

Confederation: How is the concept of "Confederation" used in the US Constitution?

Judicial Review:

Delegated, Reserved, Concurrent:

Unwritten Constitution

Filibuster

Veto, Override

Common Law

Precedent

<u>**Documents:**</u>

Mayflower Compact

Articles of Confederation: Strengths and weaknesses?

Federalist Papers

The Great Compromise

The Constitution

Bill of Rights:

Elastic Clause:

<u>Connections:</u>

Note the many ways that the concepts found in this unit are based on philosophies, and Empires in Europe.

How did Colonial Experiences affect the type of government the colonists create in the Constitution?

How did the American Revolution impact the government created by the Constitution?

How was the slavery issue handled in the US Constitution?

Highlights
Unit III: Early Tests of the Constitution.

Important People:

Jane Addams:

Susan B. Anthony:

Charles Finney:

Alexander Hamilton: (How did he create economic stability in the new nation?)

Thomas Jefferson

George Washington: (As President)

John Marshall: (List three cases and their impact.)

Daniel Webster V. John C. Calhoun

Henry Clay: Why was he known as the "Great Compromiser?"

Andrew Jackson: What is known as Jacksonian Democracy?"

Margaret Sanger:

Concepts:

Federalism: How did this change under the Marshall Court?

Federalist V. Anti-Federalist

Reservation Policy

Neutrality

Sectionalism: (Political and Cultural)

Protective Tariff: (Tariff of Abominations)

Jacksonian Democracy: What were some of the ways that Andrew Jackson attempted to make the United States more Democratic?

Scarcity

Supply and Demand

Land, Labor, Capital

Three Basic Economic Questions

Capitalism

Equilibrium Price

Immigration

Judicial Review: Also name the case that created it.

Alien-Sedition Acts

Monroe Doctrine

Supreme Court Cases

Marbury V. Madison

McCulloch V. Maryland

Connections:

What process did Alexander Hamilton use to create the National Bank? What did the Supreme Court decide about the creation of the National Bank? (Name Case)

What was created by the 10th Amendment? Early political parties clashed over the interpretation of the 10th Amendment. Describe both sides of the dispute.

By what process did Thomas Jefferson purchase the Louisiana Territory?

What principle do both Democracy and Capitalism have in common?

How did the Bill of Rights motivate many Europeans to immigrate to America?

The Federal System

National   **State**

Shared

"Delegated"   "Concurrent"   "Reserved"

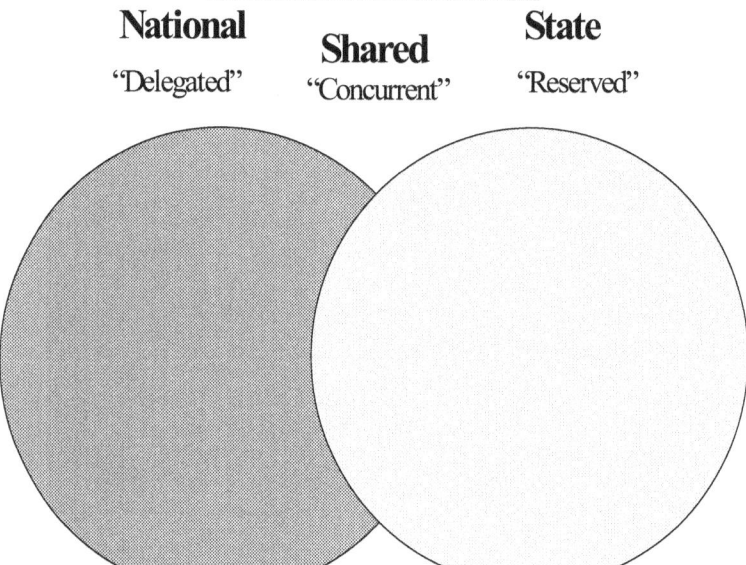

10th amend. "Powers not delegated to the federal gov't are reserved to the people and the states."

Highlights
Unit IV: The Civil War

Important People:

Henry Clay: How did his compromises contribute to causing the Civil War?

John Brown: How did his raids impact attitudes in the North and the South?

Abraham Lincoln: What were some of the techniques he used to provoke social change?

Frederick Douglass

Harriet Beecher Stowe: What did she write and what was the impact?

Ulysses S. Grant: How was he different from other commanders?

Robert E. Lee

Concepts:

Federalism: Relate this idea to the causes of the Civil War.

Sectionalism: Political and Social.

Fifth Amendment/Property Rights: Supreme Court Case?

Fanaticism: Examples.

War Powers: How did Lincoln use these powers to win the Civil War?

Reconstruction

Jim Crow Laws

Documents:

Emancipation Proclamation: What process did Lincoln use to issue it?

13th Amendment

14th Amendment: What two legal standards were established by this amendment?

15th Amendment

Gettysburg Address

Supreme Court Cases

Dred Scott V. Sanford

<u>Connections:</u>

The Civil War was fought primarily to establish that the Federal Government rules over State Governments. What amendment pertains to the issue, and Supreme Court Case dealt with this issue prior to the Civil War?

How did the development of industrialization, immigration, and urbanization accentuate the split between the North and South?

How did the Louisiana Purchase cause issues to develop between the North and South?

Highlights
Unit V: The Gilded Age.

Important People:

John D. Rockefeller

J. P. Morgan

Andrew Carnegie

Sam Gompers

Thomas Edison: What were some of his inventions/developments and what was their impact on American Society?

Henry Ford: What was his key development and what were two impacts it had on American Society?

Thomas Nast

Lewis Hine

Ida Tarbell

Upton Sinclair

Theodore Roosevelt: What was the "Square Deal", and what were some of the impacts it had on American Society?

Concepts:

The Gilded Age

Corporation: How does this legal concept affect the economy?

Trust: What are some of the good and bad impacts a trust can have on a society? Example.

Populism: What is it, and describe some of this movement's accomplishments?

Progressive Income Tax

Initiative

Referendum

Recall

17th Amendment

Collective Bargaining

Laissez Faire Economic Policy

Political Machine: What are some of the benefits and problems created by political machines? Example.

Nation

Assimilation: What inventions during the Gilded Age encouraged assimilation in the US?

Progressivism

<u>**Documents:**</u>

Pure Food and Drug Act

Meat Inspection Act

Sherman Anti-Trust Act

Court Case:

Plessey V. Ferguson

Connections:

How did Reconstruction help put America back together during the Gilded Age?

How did the Gilded Age attempt to limit the problems caused by the "Spoils System" begun under Andrew Jackson?

Graphic Representation of the Accomplishments of the Progressive Era.

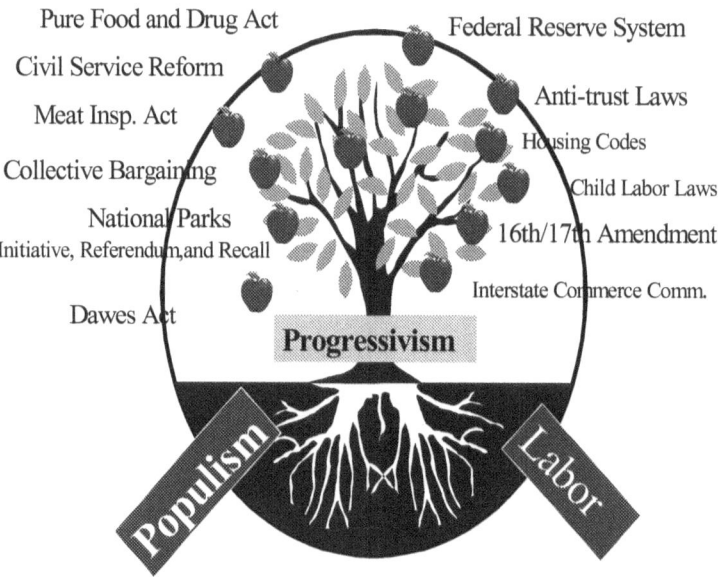

Pure Food and Drug Act
Civil Service Reform
Meat Insp. Act
Collective Bargaining
National Parks
Initiative, Referendum,and Recall
Dawes Act

Federal Reserve System
Anti-trust Laws
Housing Codes
Child Labor Laws
16th/17th Amendment
Interstate Commerce Comm.

Progressivism

Populism

Labor

Highlights
Unit VI: World War I.

Important People:

Woodrow Wilson

The Big Four

Concepts:

Nation: How does this idea connect to the Treaty of Versailles?

Nationalism: What are some examples from the pre-WWI Era?

Imperialism

Armistice: How does this differ from surrender?

Disarmament

Documents:

Zimmermann Note

The Fourteen Points

The Treaty of Versailles

Court Case:

Schenck V. USA

Connections:

How did the United States attempt to hold to its' foreign policy of neutrality prior to the First World War?

What were some of the reasons why the US Senate refused to approve the Treaty of Versailles?

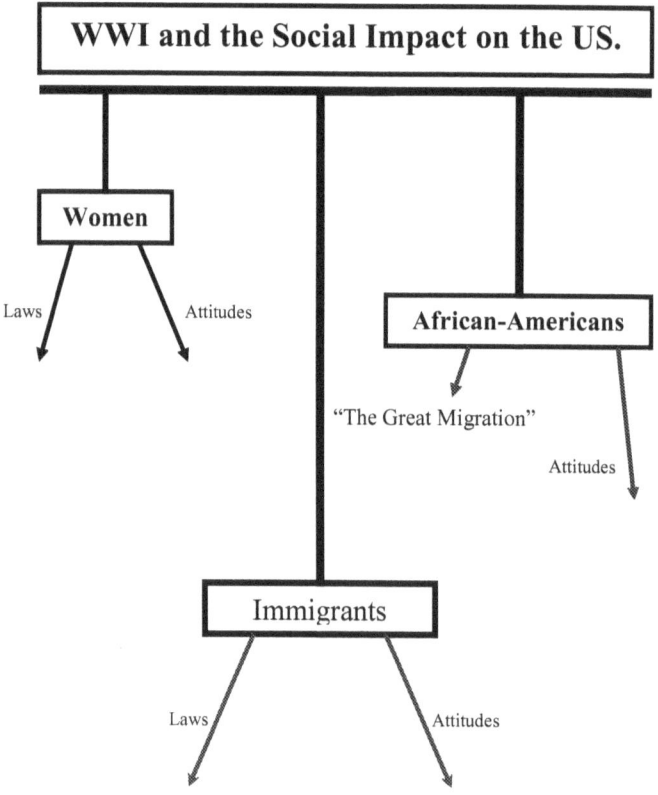

WWI and the Social Impact on the US.

Women

Laws   Attitudes

African-Americans

"The Great Migration"

Attitudes

Immigrants

Laws   Attitudes

Highlights
Unit VII: Return to Normalcy-WWII.

Important People

Herbert Hoover

Charles Lindbergh: How did he become famous and what was his impact on events leading to WWII?

Duke Ellington

Langston Hughes

Scopes (Trial)

Franklin Delano Roosevelt: What were some of the techniques he used to handle both The Great Depression and WWII?

Dwight D. Eisenhower: Impact on WWII.

George Marshall: What was his impact on WWII as well as events directly after the war?

Concepts:

Economic Interdependence: What examples of Economic interdependence are there from the 1920s, and the events that led to the Great Depression?

Tariffs

Isolationism: How did America try to follow this policy leading up to WWII?

Women's suffrage

Judicial Review: Describe two examples from this time period.

Imperialism

Nationalism

Appeasement

Nuremberg Trials

Yalta Conference

Cold War: The beginnings.

Documents

Treaty of Versailles: What were some of the ways that the Treaty of Versailles impacted the 1920s and 1930s?

Washington Conference: What was its impact on the rise of fascism in the 1930s?

19th Amendment

The New Deal: Identify three goals of this package of programs as well as describe three key programs.

Good Neighbor Policy

Executive Order 9066

United Nations Charter

N.A.T.O.

Marshall Plan

<u>Supreme Court Cases</u>

Schechter Poultry Corporation V. USA (1936)

Korematsu V. USA (1944)

Connections

How do both the Great Depression and WWII connect to the Treaty of Versailles that ended WWI?

How are the causes of the Great Depression and Triangular Trade similar?

How are Theodore Roosevelt and Franklin Roosevelt's policies toward Latin America different?

In what ways did "Checks and Balances" limit Franklin Roosevelt's power?

Highlights
Unit VIII: Cold War.

Important People

Harry Truman

Joseph McCarthy

Edward R. Murrow

Dwight Eisenhower

John Foster Dulles

John F. Kennedy

Lyndon B. Johnson

Richard Nixon

Henry Kissinger

Baby Boom

Concepts

Cold War

Containment

Domino Theory

Documents

The Fair Deal

The GI Bill

Truman Doctrine

Eisenhower Doctrine

S.E.A.T.O.

The New Frontier

Alliance for Progress

The Great Society

Civil Rights Act 1965

Voting Rights Act 1965

Pentagon Papers

War Powers Act 1973

Supreme Court Cases

New York Times V. USA 1971

Connections

How is the War Powers Act 1973 an example of the use of checks and balances?

In ways are the roots of the Cold War found in the events of WWII?

How did Television impact both the McCarthy Hearings and the Vietnam War?

How are SEATO and NATO similar and different?

How is the "Alliance for Progress" similar to "The Good Neighbor Policy?"

How is the "Great Society" similar to the "New Deal?"

How are the Vietnam and Korean Wars similar and different?

FDR implemented war powers in order to take complete charge of the government during WWII. Why did presidents during the Vietnam War not do the same?

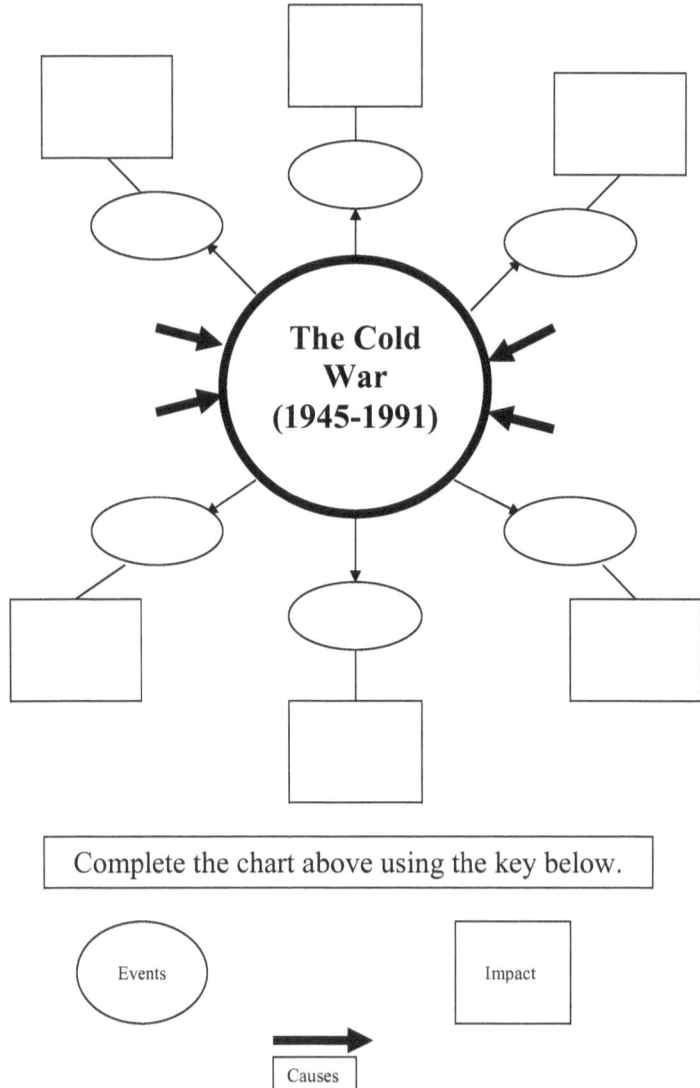

The Cold War (1945-1991)

Complete the chart above using the key below.

Events

Impact

Causes

Highlights
Unit IX Civil Rights.

Important People

Harry Truman: What was his impact on race relations in the US?

Earl Warren: What were some common themes found in his Supreme Court decisions?

Thurgood Marshall

Rosa Parks

Martin Luther King Jr. What were some the techniques Dr. King used to provoke social change? Examples.

Jackie Robinson

W.E.B. Dubois: (Title of Significant Book)

Booker T. Washington: (Title of Significant Book)

Malcolm X

Ida B. Wells-Barnett

Concepts

Segregation V. Integration

The president influences the Supreme Court based on his appointments.

Federalism: What role did federalism play in the Civil Rights Era?

Civil Disobedience

Black Nationalism

Harlem Renaissance

Right to Privacy

Reservation Policy

Equal Protection Under the Law using Due Process

<u>**Documents**</u>

GI Bill

Civil Rights Act 1965

Voting Rights Act 1965

14th Amendment

Title IX

Supreme Court Cases

Plessey V. Ferguson 1896

Brown V. The Board of Education of Topeka, Kansas 1954

Engle v. Vitale 1962

Gideon V. Wainwright 1963

Miranda V. Arizona 1966

Roe V. Wade 1973

New Jersey V. TLO 1985

Connections

How did the passing of the GI Bill after WWII inspire a revival of Civil Rights in the 1950s?

How did President Truman attempt to provoke social change in America during the Korean War?

How did President Eisenhower try to influence the Supreme Court during the Civil Rights Era?

How did the decision in the Supreme Court case of Brown V. The Board of Education of Topeka, Kansas 1954 change the legal interpretation of the 14th Amendment?

How is President Eisenhower's sending of troops into Little Rock, Ark. a good example of federalism?

How is President Kennedy's sending of troops to the University of Alabama is a good example federalism?

Black Nationalism has its root in ideas and events before WWII. What were some of those connections?

Women Rights was greatly expanded by the 19th Amendment passed in 1920 that gave women suffrage.

Highlights
Unit X: Recent Challenges.

Important People

Richard Nixon

Sam Ervin

Gerald Ford: How did he try to heal the nation after both Watergate and the Vietnam War?

Woodward and Bernstein

Jimmy Carter

Ronald Reagan

Colin Powell

Détente

Ping Pong Diplomacy

Recognition: Name an example from this unit.

Executive Privilege

Judicial Review: What examples of judicial review were applied in this unit?

Presidential Pardon

Boycott

Federalism: Examples from this unit.

Budget Deficits

Documents

SEATO

Nixon Doctrine

S.A.L.T.

O.P.E.C. Name several member nations.

Human Rights Policy

E.P.A.

Freedom of Information Act 1974

Camp David Accords 1978

Reagan's "New Federalism"

N.A.F.T.A.

<u>**Supreme Court Cases**</u>

New York Times V. USA 1971

USA V. Nixon 1974

Bush V. Gore 2001

Connections

How does the Nixon Doctrine alter our obligations under SEATO? When was it applied?

How did checks and balances ultimately limit the power of President Nixon?

How did checks and balances ultimately limit the power of President Clinton?

How does President Carter's foreign policy of "Human Rights" compare to "isolation?"

How did President Reagan alter the relationship between the federal government and state governments?

How might our continuing problems in the Middle East be related to the Eisenhower Doctrine as well as Economic Interdependence?

How are Ronald Reagan's foreign policies similar to that of Theodore Roosevelt's?

The Presidency.

I. Essential Presidencies for the Exam:

a. George Washington (1789-1797)

Challenges: First President, Troubles with France, and the New Economy.

Events: Creation of the National Bank, Organized the Cabinet, Whiskey Rebellion, and Termination of Alliance with France.

Documents/Policies: Isolationism, Farewell Address.

Impact: Two-Term Presidency, Creation of Cabinet.

b. Thomas Jefferson (1801-1809)

Challenges: National Unity and European meddling in domestic affairs.

Events: Louisiana Purchase, and the expiration of the Alien-Sedition Acts.

Documents: Treaty to acquire Louisiana Territory.

Impact: Expanded the power of the president by purchasing Louisiana.

c. Andrew Jackson (1829-1837)

Challenges: Excessive power in the hands of the elite.

Events: Enforcement of Tariff Laws, persistent vetoing of Southern Legislation, and the "Trail of Tears."

Documents/Policies: Opened voting to non-property owners, dismantling of National Bank, "Spoils System", and the Reservation policy toward Native-Americans.

Impact: Expanded the power of the presidency through his veto power, increased suffrage for the poor, and managed economic issues.

d. Abraham Lincoln (1861-1865)

Challenges: Restore the Union.

Events: Civil War (1861-1965)

Documents/Speeches: Emancipation Proclamation, Gettysburg Address, and the Second Inaugural Address.

Impact: Expanded the War Powers of the Presidency-Draft, Income Tax, and suspension of habeas corpus, and freed the slaves.

e. Theodore Roosevelt (1901-1909)

Challenges: Balance the interests of big business with the interest of the public.

Events: Building of the Panama Canal, Breaking apart of Standard Oil, creation of the National Parks and National Forests System, building of a modern US Navy.

Documents/Policies: Passing of Pure Food and Drug Act (1906), Meat Inspection Act (1906), Square Deal, and the Roosevelt Corollary to the Monroe Doctrine.

Impact: Expanded America's influence in the world, and expanded the economic and social role of the president.

f. Woodrow Wilson (1913-1921).

Challenges: Winning WWI and negotiating the Treaty of Versailles.

Events: World War I (1914-1919), the Versailles Negotiation, and the rejection of the Treaty of Versailles by the US Senate.

Documents/Policies: Anti-Child Labor Laws, the Fourteen Points, the Treaty of Versailles, and the 19th Amendment establishing Women's Suffrage.

Impact: America established a world leader, and democracy expanded to include women.

g. Franklin Delano Roosevelt (1933-1945)

Challenges: The Great Depression and World War II.

Events: Great Depression, Pearl Harbor, Schechter Poultry Corporation V. USA (1936), Korematsu V. USA (1944), and World War II.

Documents/Policies/Legislation: New Deal, Executive Order 9066, Court Packing, and Good Neighbor Policy.

Impact: Ended the Great Depression, and won World War II. Expanded the war powers of the president, and created the modern bureaucratic presidency.

h. Harry S. Truman (1945-1953)

Challenges: Ending World War II, and the start of the Cold War.

Events: Dropping of the atomic bomb on Japan, formation of the United Nations, and the start of the Korean War (1950-1953).

Documents/Policies: Fair Deal, Integration of the armed forces, Truman Doctrine, and the Marshall Plan.

i. John F. Kennedy (1961-1963)

Challenges: Soviet Influence in Western
Hemisphere, communist influence in Southeast Asia, and US Civil Rights.

Events: Bay of Pigs Invasion, Cuban Missile Crisis, integration of the
Universities of Alabama and Mississippi, and Nuclear Test Ban Treaty.

Documents/Policy: New Frontier, Alliance for Progress, proposed the Civil
Rights Act, and the Voting Rights Act.

Impact: President as advocate for Civil Rights, and combat troops in
Vietnam.

j. Nixon Presidency (1969-1974)

Challenges: Vietnam War, Soviet/Chinese relations
with the US, and the Watergate Scandal.

Events: Bombings of Cambodia, Paris Peace Conference ending the
Vietnam War, Ping-Pong Diplomacy with China, Détente' with USSR,
Watergate Break-In, Congressional Investigation, USA V. Nixon, and
resignation.

Documents/Policies: Nixon Doctrine, War Powers Act (vetoed by Nixon),
and recognition of China.

Impact: Weakened Presidency, and weakened ability of the president to
conduct war.

k. Ronald Reagan (1981-1989)

Challenges: Economic Recession, Budget
Deficits, and an Invigorated Soviet Union.

Events: Tax Cuts, Increasing Budget Deficits, and Summits with USSR.

Documents/Policies: New Federalism, and Supply-Side Economics.

Impact: Reform in USSR, and the Presidency used as an economic
manager.

l. George Bush (1989-1993)

Challenges: Budget Deficits, Gulf War, and
Collapse of the USSR.

Events: The Collapse of the USSR (1991), and the United Nations Action in
the Gulf War (1991).

Documents/Policies: Use of the United Nations in Post-Cold War events,
and the recognition of newly independent states from the collapse of the
USSR.

Impact: Continuing U.S. military involvement in the Middle East.

m. Bill Clinton (1993-2001)

Challenges: Budget Deficits, and then Surpluses, Growing Terrorism, and Impeachment.

Events: Impeachment by the House of Representatives.

Documents/Policies: North American Free Trade Agreement (NAFTA).

Impact: Strong Economy, and an Empowered Congress.

n. George W. Bush (2001-2009)

Challenges: Controversial Election (2001), 911 Terrorism, Recession, Budget Deficits, Prolonged Wars in Afghanistan, and Iraq.

Events: 911 Terrorism, Bush v. Gore (2001), Wars in Afghnaistan and Iraq.

Documents/Policies: Bush Doctrine, and Patriot Act.

Impact: Prolonged wars in Afghanistan and Iraq. A Democratic Congress.

Domestic Agendas

Jeffersonian Democracy:

How did Thomas Jefferson make America more of a Democracy?

Jacksonian Democracy:

Identify two ways Andrew Jackson helped more people participate in government?

Theodore Roosevelt's "Square Deal":

List a few ways in which Theodore Roosevelt protected average Americans from abuses by Big Business.

Franklin Roosevelt's "New Deal":

What crisis was the "New Deal created to solve?

What were the three "R's" the New Deal attempted to achieve?

Identify at least three programs created by the New Deal, and briefly describe each programs goal.

Harry Truman's "Fair Deal":

Describe two ways in which Truman used the military to distribute America's prosperity to people of color.

John F. Kennedy's "New Frontier":

Describe at least two ways in which JFK tried to expand the participation of young Americans in America's future?

Lyndon Johnson's "Great Society":

How did the "Great Society" attack the problems of poverty and race relations in the US?

Ronald Reagan's "New Federalism":

In what ways did Ronald Reagan attempt to shift power back to the state and local governments?

Foreign Policies

Isolationism: Begun by George Washington. USA should avoid problems in Europe unless directly attacked.

Example...

Washington did not assist France during their revolutions.

Monroe Doctrine (1823): James Monroe. USA will dominate the Western Hemisphere and prevent European Powers from establishing colonies.

Examples...

US involvement in the Spanish-American War 1898 (McKinley)

Cuban Missile Crisis 1962 (Kennedy)

Invasion of Panama 1989 (Bush I)

Roosevelt Corollary to the Monroe Doctrine (1904): Theodore Roosevelt. USA had a right to intervene in Latin America-backed up by the building of the Panama Canal and the new 100-battleship navy. Also known as the "Big Stick" policy.

Examples...

Building of the Panama Canal 1904 (Theodore Roosevelt)

Bay of Pigs Invasion 1961 (Kennedy)

Good Neighbor Policy (1930-1945 Hoover/Franklin Roosevelt) **US** will attempt to improve relations with Latin America by treating them as equals.

Examples...

Withdraw of US troops from Nicaragua 1931 (Hoover)

Truman encouraged Latin American Nations to join the United Nations after WWII.

The Truman Doctrine (1947): US will attempt to defeat communism by stopping it from spreading to any more countries. "Containment"

Examples...

Korean War 1950-1953 (Truman/Eisenhower)

Berlin Airlift (1948 Truman)

Vietnam War (1961-1973 Kennedy/Johnson/Nixon)

Eisenhower Doctrine (1957) It was an extension of the Truman Doctrine into the Middle East. US will support all pro-western countries in the Middle East.

Examples...

US Support of King Hussein of Jordan

US Support of Israel

US Support of the Shah of Iran

Nixon Doctrine (1973 Nixon/Ford): US will support our Allies in Southeast Asia, but no US troops will be involved. "No more Vietnams."

Example...

US does not intervene militarily when South Vietnam Falls in 1975.

Bush Doctrine (2001): USA reserves the right to preemptively strike countries involved in terrorist activities.

Examples...

US invasion of Afghanistan

US Invasion of Iraq

War: The Bare Bones...

American Revolution (1775-1781)

The Civil War (1861-1865) Lincoln:

WWI (1917-1919) Wilson:

WWII (1941-1945) FDR/Truman:

Korean War (1950-1953) Truman/Eisenhower:

Vietnam (1963-1973) JFK/Johnson/Nixon:

Gulf War (1991) George Bush:

Enduring Freedom/War on Terrorism (2002-Present) George W. Bush:

Complete the chart below…

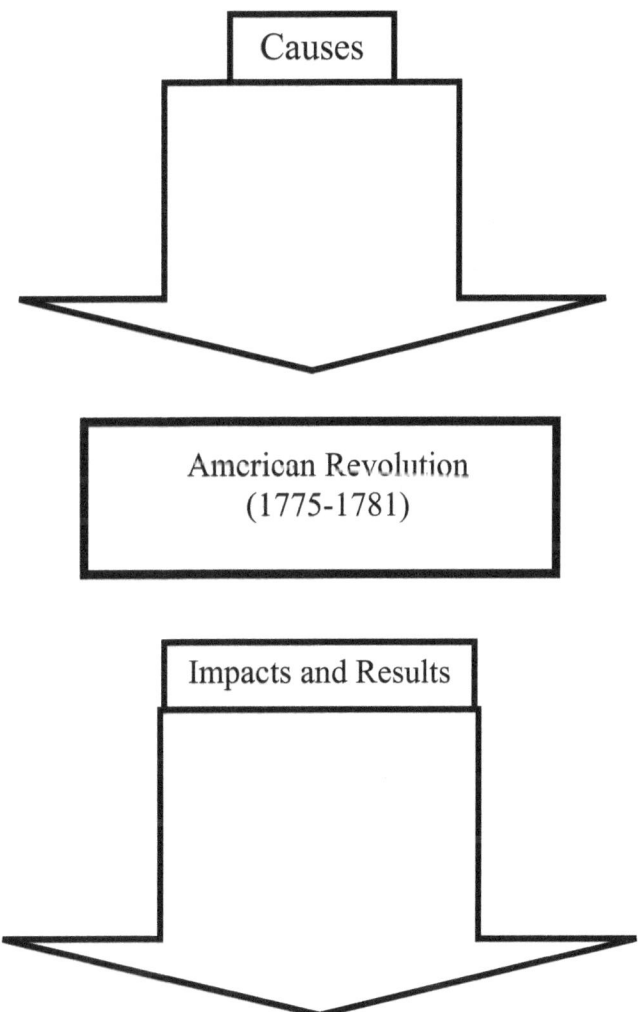

Causes

American Revolution
(1775-1781)

Impacts and Results

Complete the chart below...

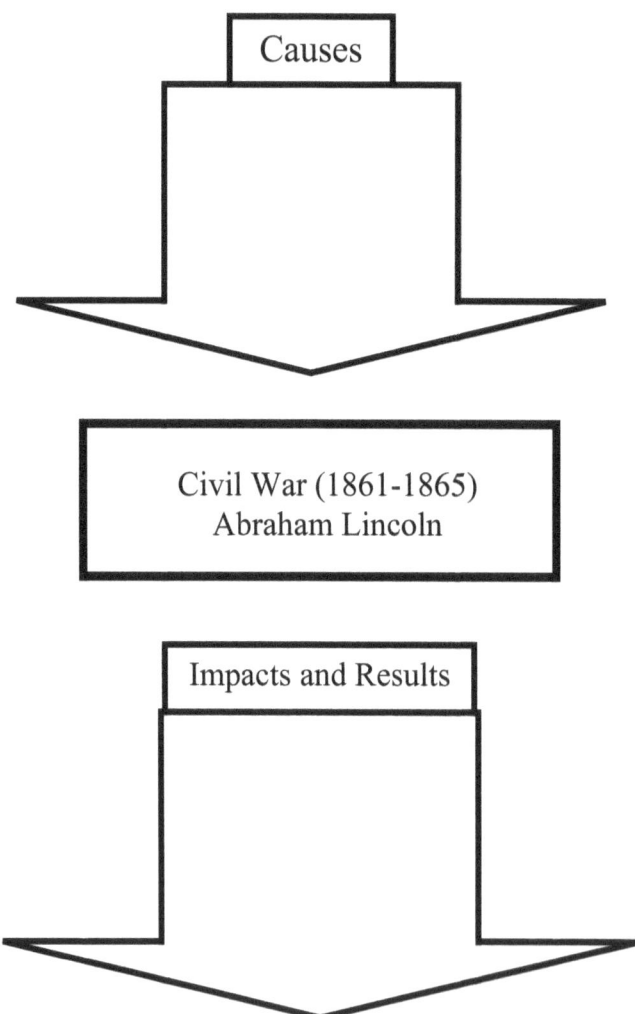

Causes

Civil War (1861-1865)
Abraham Lincoln

Impacts and Results

Complete the chart below…

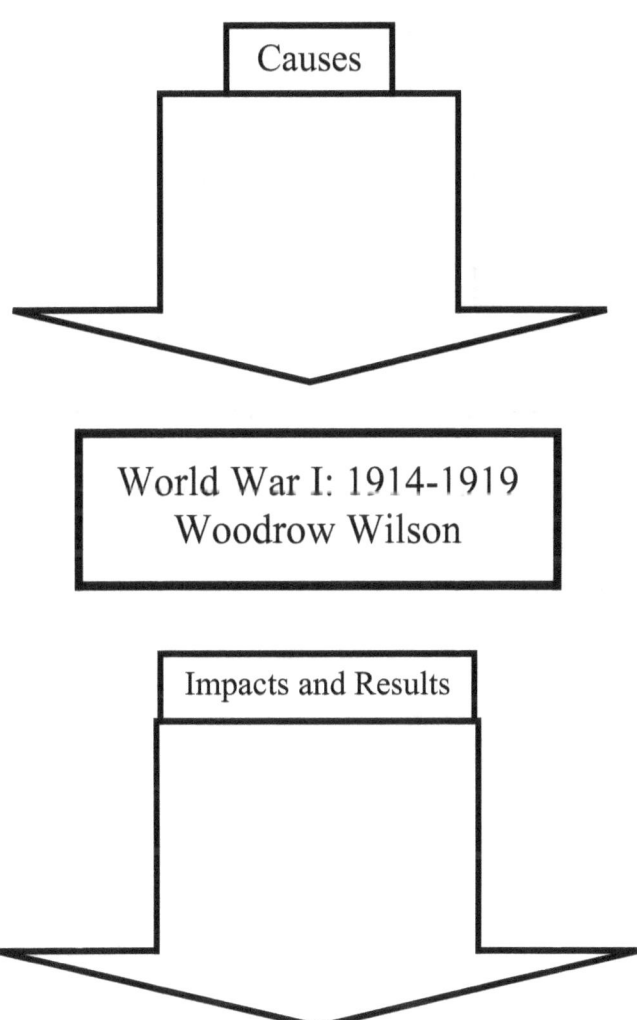

Causes

World War I: 1914-1919
Woodrow Wilson

Impacts and Results

Complete the chart below…

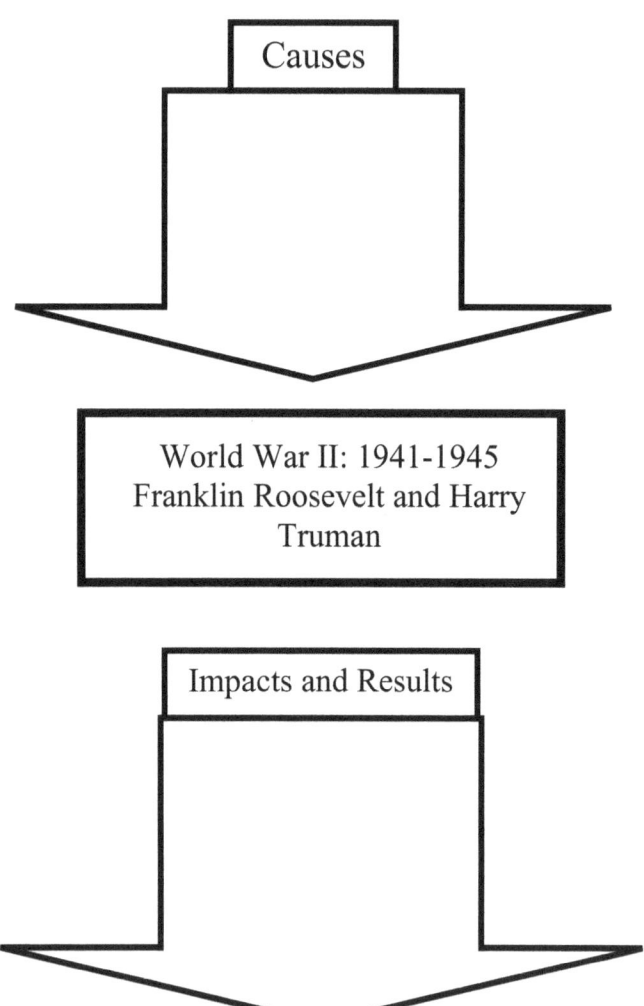

Causes

World War II: 1941-1945
Franklin Roosevelt and Harry
Truman

Impacts and Results

Complete the chart below…

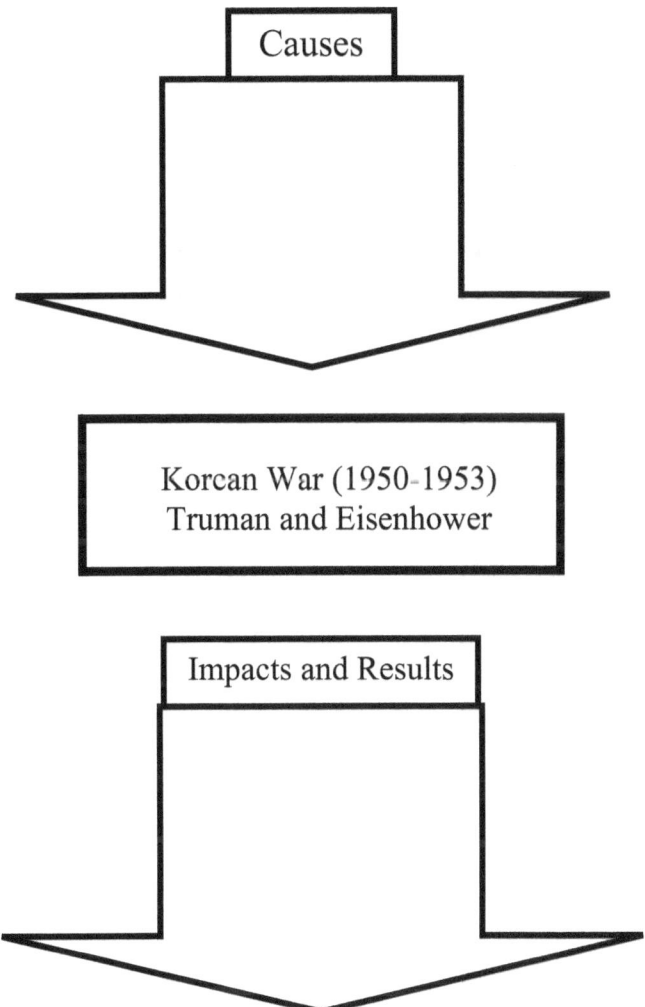

Causes

Korcan War (1950-1953)
Truman and Eisenhower

Impacts and Results

Complete the chart below…

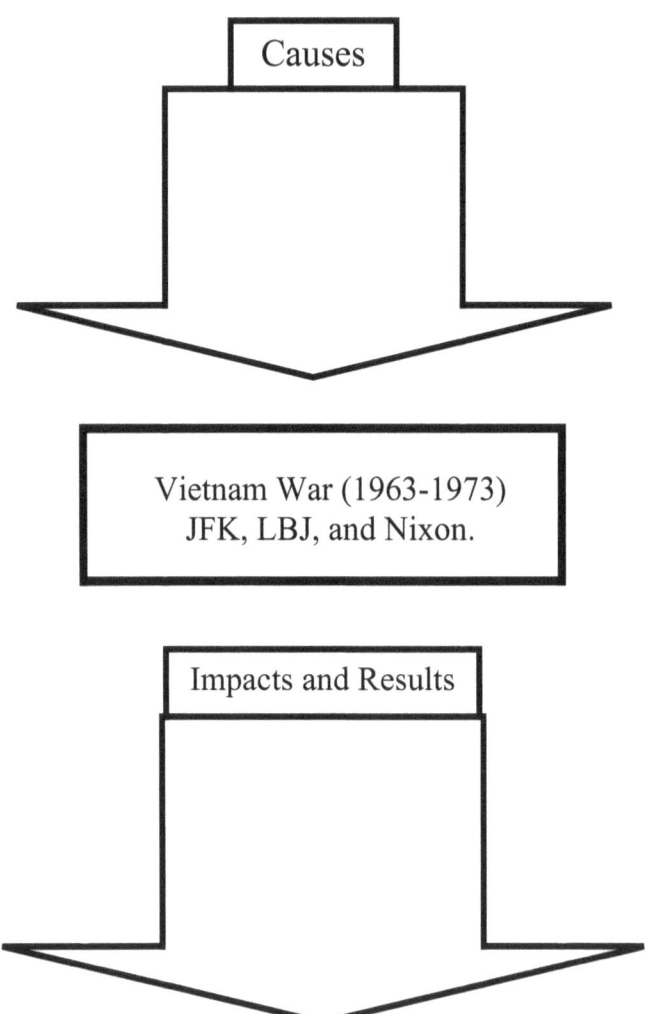

Causes

Vietnam War (1963-1973)
JFK, LBJ, and Nixon.

Impacts and Results

Complete the chart below…

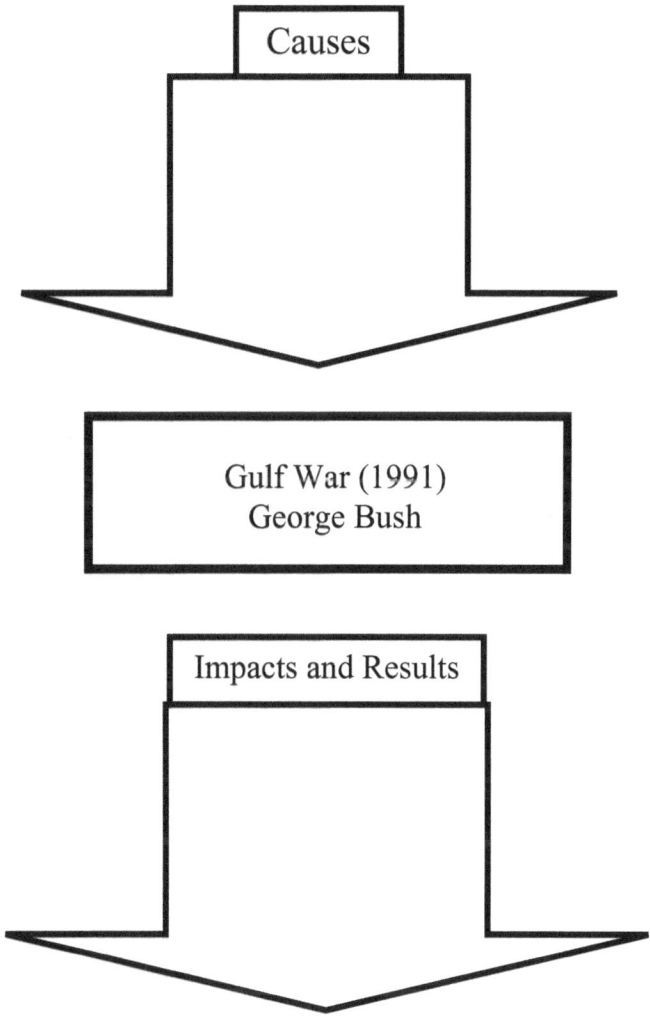

Causes

Gulf War (1991)
George Bush

Impacts and Results

Complete the chart below…

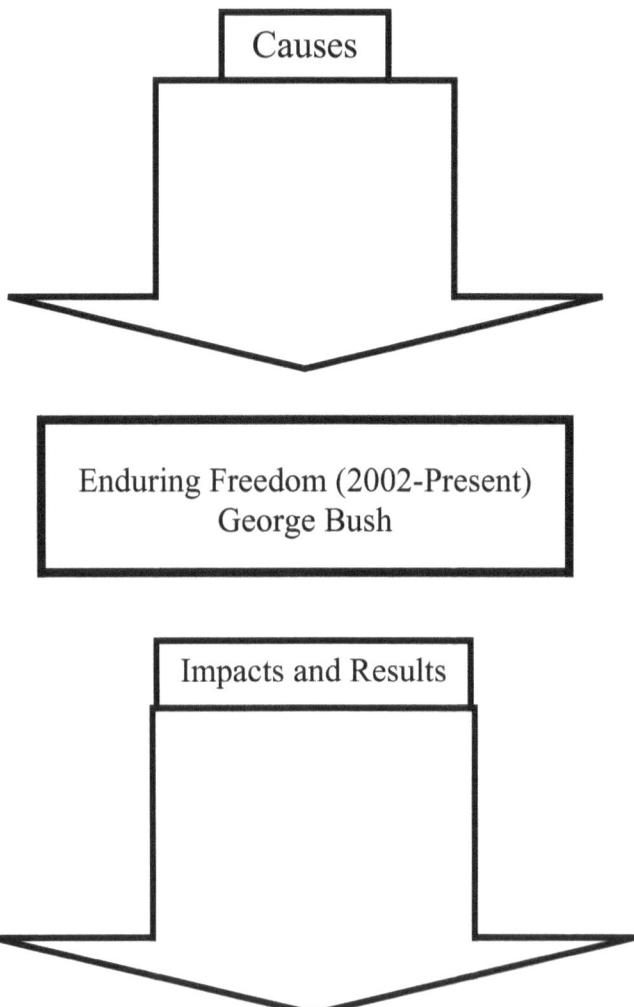

Causes

Enduring Freedom (2002-Present)
George Bush

Impacts and Results

Checks on the Presidency

Marbury v. Madison (1803)

Impeachment Hearings on Andrew Johnson (1868)

Schenck v. USA (1919)

Schechter Poultry Corporation v. USA (1936)

Korematsu v. USA (1944)

Impeachment Hearings for President Richard Nixon (1974)

Override of President Nixon's veto of the War Powers Act (1974)

USA v. Nixon (1974)

Impeachment of President Bill Clinton (1999)

Documents, Legislation, and Congressional

Actions...

Documents

Magna Carta (1215)

The Great Compromise (1787)

The Iroquois Confederacy

Bill of Rights (1791)

Mayflower Compact (1620)

Alien and Sedition Acts (1798)

Declaration of Independence (1776)

Missouri Compromise (1820)

Articles of Confederation (1781)

Fugitive Slave Act (1850)

US Constitution (1789)

Kansas-Nebraska Act (1854)

Emancipation Proclamation (1863)	**Meat Inspection Act (1906)**
Homestead Act (1862)	**Pure Food and Drug Act (1906)**
Interstate Commerce Act (1887)	**Fourteen Points (1918)**
Chinese Exclusion Act (1882)	**Kellogg-Briand Pact (1928)**
Dawes Act (1887)	**Hawley-Smoot Tariff (1930)**
Sherman Anti-Trust Act (1890)	**Lend-Lease Act (1941)**

Executive Order 9066 (1942)	Gulf of Tonkin Resolution (1964)
Interstate Highway Act (1956)	Pentagon Papers (1971)
Civil Rights Act (1964)	Equal Employment Opportunity Act (1972)
Voting Rights Act (1964)	Vocational Rehabilitation Act (1973)

<u>Important Congressional Actions:</u>

Amendments of Consequence:

Bill of Rights: First Ten Amendments...

1.

2.

4.

5. (Five Parts)

6.

7.

8.

10.

Define: Delegated, Reserved, and Concurrent.

Amendments…

    13.

    14.

    15.

    16.

    17.

    19.

Approval of Appointments with historical consequences:

Approval of John Marshall as Chief Justice.

Approval of Earl Warren as Chief Justice.

Legislation:

Passage of New Deal Programs: (Name a Few)

G.I. Bill after WWII:

Civil Rights Act 1965: What law did this expand on?

Voting Rights Act 1965:

Passage of Reagan Tax Cuts:

Patriot Act:

Treaties:

Rejection of the Treaty of Versailles:

Treaty to Purchase Louisiana:

Creation of the United Nations:

N.A.T.O:

S.A.L.T.

N.A.F.T.A.

Declarations for war:

Declaration of War in WWI or WWII:

Gulf of Tonkin Resolution:

Approval of Gulf War:

Approval of Operation Enduring Freedom:

Check and Balances Issues:

Marbury V. Madison (1803):

Impeachment hearings on Andrew Johnson:

Schenck V. USA (1919):

Schechter Poultry Corporation V. USA (1936):

Korematsu V. USA:

Impeachment hearings for Richard Nixon:

Impeachment of Bill Clinton: (Not removed by the Senate)

Override of Nixon's Veto of the War Powers Act:

USA V. Nixon:

Override of Reagan's Veto of Dr. King's Birthday as a national holiday:

US Supreme Court Cases: Bare Bone…

Supreme Court Cases...

Marbury V. Madison (1803) Marshall-Created Judicial Review. Checks and Balances.

McCulloch V. Maryland (1819) Marshall-Federalism and Elastic Clause. Checks and Balances. Use of Judicial Review. Tenth Amendment.

Gibbons V. Ogden (1824) Marshall- Federalism. Tenth Amendment.

Dred Scott V. Sanford (1857) Taney- Status of slaves. Provokes Civil War. Property Rights. Fifth Amendment.

Plessy V. Ferguson (1896) Brown- Separate can be Equal. 14th Amendment.

Schenck V. USA (1919) Oliver Wendell Holmes- "Clear and Present Danger." Expansion of War Powers and limits on the 1st Amendment.

Schechter Poultry Corporation V. USA (1935) Hughes- "No War Powers during a domestic crisis." Dismantled NRA and other parts of New Deal.

Korematsu V. USA (1944) Hughes- Internment of Japanese is Legal/War Powers. Fifth Amendment.

Brown V. The Board of Education of Topeka, Kansas (1954) Warren- "Separate Cannot Be Equal" 14th Amendment.

Engel V. Vitale (1962) Warren- Organized School Prayer a violation of separation of chruch and state   First Amendment.

Gideon V. Wainwright (1963) Warren- Right to Counsel. Sixth Amendment.

Miranda V. Arizona (1966) Warren- Informed of Rights. Fifth Amendment.

Tinker V. Des Moines (1969) Warren-Freedom of Speech does apply within schools-unless is a threat to maintaining order. First Amendment.

New York Times Co. V. United States (1971) Berger- Right to Print the Pentagon Papers was covered under the First Amendment.

Roe V. Wade (1973) Berger- Right to Abortion as a right to privacy. Fourth Amendment.

USA V. Nixon (1974) Berger- "Executive Privilege" does not apply in a criminal investigation.

University of California Regents at Berkley V. Bakke (1978) Affirmative Action is not a violation of one's Fourteenth Amendment Rights.

New Jersey V. T.L.O. (1985) Students do have a "right to privacy" within a school. Fourth Amendment.

Clinton V. New York City (1998) Rehnquist- End of the Line-Item Veto. Separation of Powers.

Bush V. Gore (2001) Rehnquist- Asserted local control of Election Procedures. Additional recount would violate the 14th Amendment to the Constitution and its "Equal protection under law."

I. <u>Lists...</u>

a. People to know.

b. Books to Remember.

Important People:

Jane Addams

Susan B. Anthony

Louis Armstrong

Rachel Carson

Dorthea Dix

Frederick Douglass

W.E.B. Dubois

John Foster Dulles

Thomas Edison

Duke Ellington

Medgar Evers

Charles Finney

Henry Ford

Betty Freidan

William Lloyd Garrison

Marcus Garvey

Samuel Gompers

Alexander Hamilton

Patrick Henry

Langston Hughes

Thomas Jefferson

Martin Luther King Jr.

Henry Kissinger

Robert LaFollette

Charles Lindbergh

John Locke

Douglas MacArthur

James Madison

Malcolm X

George Marshall

John Marshall

Thurgood Marshall

Joseph McCarthy

James Meredith

Baron de Montesquieu

J.P. Morgan

Lucrecia Mott

John Muir

Thomas Paine

Rosa Parks

Commodore Mathew Perry

Jacob Riis

Jackie Robinson

John D. Rockefeller

Eleanor Roosevelt

Jean-Jacques Rousseau

Babe Ruth

Colin Powell

Margaret Sanger

John Scopes

Upton Sinclair

Elizabeth Cady Stanton

Lincoln Steffens

Gloria Steinem

Ida Tarbell

Sojourner Truth

Harriet Tubman

Nat Turner

Earl Warren

Booker T. Washington

Daniel Webster

Ida B. Wells-Barnet

Important Books

The Narrative of the Life of Frederick Douglass: by Frederick Douglass (1845)

Uncle Tom's Cabin: Harriet Beecher Stowe (1852)

Walden: by Henry David Thoreau (1854)

The Gilded Age: by Mark Twain (1873)

How the Other Half Lives: by Jacob Riis (1890)

Up From Slavery: by Booker T. Washington (1901)

The Souls of Black Folk: by W.E.B. Dubois (1903)

The Shame of the Cities: by Lincoln Steffens (1904)

History of Standard Oil: by Ida Tarbell (1904)

The Jungle: by Upton Sinclair (1906)

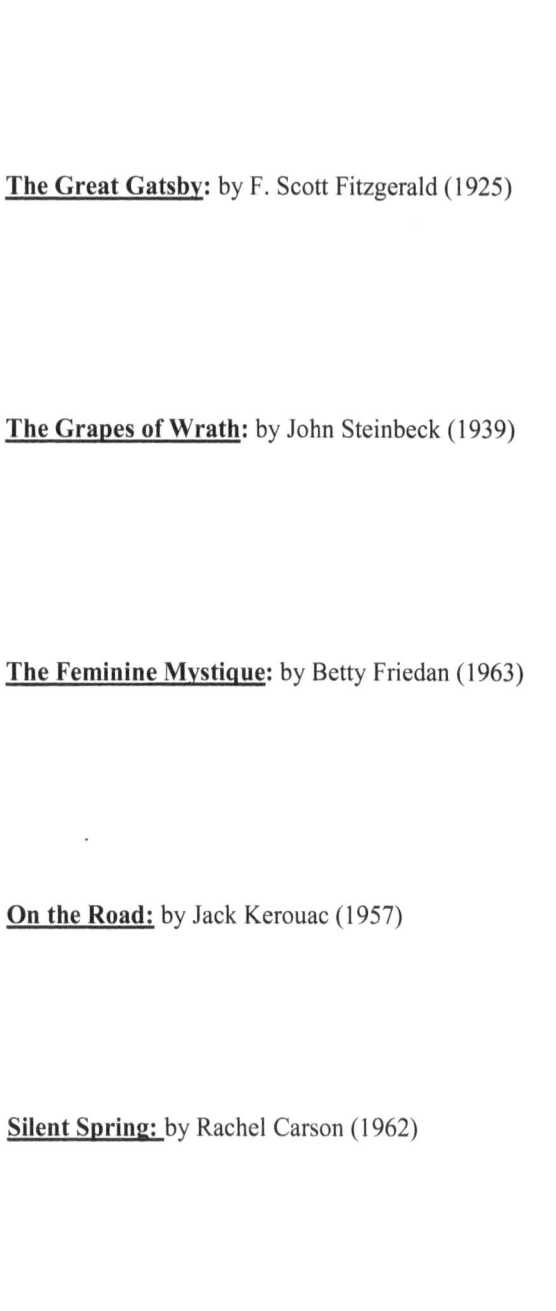

The Great Gatsby: by F. Scott Fitzgerald (1925)

The Grapes of Wrath: by John Steinbeck (1939)

The Feminine Mystique: by Betty Friedan (1963)

.

On the Road: by Jack Kerouac (1957)

Silent Spring: by Rachel Carson (1962)

Unsafe at any Speed: by Ralph Nader (1965)

Terms

Abolitionism

Accommodation

Anarchism

Appeasement

Armistice

Arsenal

Assimilate

Baby Boom

Black Nationalism

Terms

Blacklisting

Boycott

Brinksmanship Diplomacy

Business Cycle

Censure

Checks and Balances

Communism

Confederacy

Terms

Containment

Default

Deficit

Democratization

Depression

Desegregation

Détente

Disarmament

Dissention

Terms

Domino Theory

Double Jeopardy

Due Process

Dynamic Scoring of a Budget

Elastic Clause

Emancipation

Eminent Domain

Equilibrium Price

Executive Privilege

<u>Terms</u>

Fanaticism

Federalism

Great Migration

Habeas Corpus

Human Rights Policy

Impeach

Imperialism

<u>Terms</u>

Implied Powers

Impoverished

Inaugural

Integration

Interdependence

Internment

Iron Curtain

Terms

Island-Hopping

Isolationism

Judicial Review

Laissez Faire

Landslide

Law of Comparative Advantage

Manifest Destiny

McCarthyism

Mercantilism

Terms

Militarism

Mobilization

Monarchy

Nation

Nationalism

Nativism

Natural Rights

Non-recognition

Normalcy

Terms

Opportunity Cost

Override

Presidential Pardon

Perjury

Ping-Pong Diplomacy

Political Machine

Populism

Prohibition

Quarantine

Terms

Realpolitik

Recession

Recognition

Reparations

Salutary Neglect

Scarcity

Sectionalism

Segregated

Self-Incrimination

<u>Terms</u>

Socialism

Spoils System

Stalemate

Static Scoring of a Budget

Suffrage

Supply and Demand

Supply-Side Economics

Tariff

Terms

Temperance

Triangulated Foreign Policy

Trusts

Viability

Viet Cong

Vietnamization

Yellow Press

www.ingramcontent.com/pod-product-compliance
Lightning Source LLC
Chambersburg PA
CBHW051437280526
45785CB00003B/1317